PARENT-FREE ZONE

Brian Moses lives in Sussex with his wife and
two daughters. Since first becoming a parent
ten years ago he has lost a lot of sleep, a lot
of hair and a lot of patience.

Lucy Maddison lives in Balham, London,
with Pup the cat.

Also available from Macmillan

THE SECRET LIVES OF TEACHERS
Revealing Rymes chosen by Brian Moses

'ERE WE GO!
Football Poems
chosen by David Orme

YOU'LL NEVER WALK ALONE
More Football Poems chosen by David Orme

DRACULA'S AUNTIE RUTHLESS
and other Petrifying Poems chosen by David Orme

SNOGGERS Slap 'n' Tickle Poems
chosen by David Orme

NOTHING TASTES QUITE LIKE A GERBIL
and other vile verses
chosen by David Orme

PARENT-FREE ZONE

ZONE

Poems about parents
and other problems

CHOSEN BY
BRIAN MOSES

ILLUSTRATED BY
LUCY MADDISON

MACMILLAN CHILDREN'S BOOKS

'Children begin by loving their parents;
after a time they judge them;
rarely, if ever, do they forgive them.'
Oscar Wilde

First published 1997 by
Macmillan Children's Books
a division of Macmillan Publishers Ltd
25 Eccleston Place, London SW1W 9NF
and Basingstoke

Associated companies throughout the world

ISBN 0 330 34554 0

1 3 5 7 9 8 6 4 2

A CIP catalogue record for this book is available from the British Library.

Printed by Mackays of Chatham plc, Chatham, Kent.

CONTENTS

Urgent Note to my Parents

Don't ask me to do what I can't do
Only ask me to do what I can
Don't ask me to be what I can't be
Only ask me to be what I am

Don't one minute say 'Be a big girl'
And the next 'You're too little for that'
PLEASE don't ask me to be where I can't be
PLEASE be happy with right where I'm at

Hiawyn Oram

The Good Parent Guide: Kids in a Huff
The Standard Apology Template

Dear _____(fill in name)
Your mother and I think it would be nice
if we could meet up sometime in
the future ☐ the kitchen ☐ the hope that we
remember what you look like ☐
We know we always complained about
your loud music ☐ your hairstyle ☐ having
children ☐
But now we're sorry and want to call
a truce ☐ a cab ☐ a meeting ☐
Perhaps we should
get together ☐ get away ☐ get a life ☐
We really miss you, especially your
sense of humour ☐ sense of style ☐
total lack of sense ☐
And anyway
Grandma ☐ the hamster ☐ the kitchen table ☐
is pining for you.
So get in touch
by letter ☐ by pigeon ☐ by tea-time ☐
Your loving parents
_____and_____.

Jane Wright
(Tick boxes as applicable)

W-W-W-W-Why?

Why do parents make life a pain?

Whatever I do
        I'm wrong, again.
Whomever I'm with
        they're bad for me.
Wherever I am
        I shouldn't be.
Whenever I *want*
        there is no time.

How did I ever get parents like mine?

Gina Douthwaite

Lovey-Dovey

When Dad and Mum go all lovey-dovey
we just don't know where to look.
My sister says, 'Cut it out you two,'
while I stick my nose in a book.

Mum has this faraway look on her face
while Dad has a silly grin.
'You don't have to mind us, kids,' he says.
We just wish they'd pack it in.

Dad calls Mum, 'Little Sugarplum'
and Mum says, 'You handsome brute'.
Dad laughs and says, 'Look at your Mum,
don't you think that she's cute?'

'I guess that's why I married her,
she's my truly wonderful one.'
Mum says he doesn't mean any of it
but she thinks he's a lot of fun.

I just can't stand all the kissing,
at their age they ought to know better.
I think I'll go up to my room
and write *Jim'll Fix It* a letter.

I hate it when they're lovey-dovey
but I hate it more when they fight
when faces redden and tempers flare
and sharp words cut through the night.

I'd rather they kissed and cuddled
and joked about and laughed,
at least we can tell everything's OK
when Mum and Dad are daft.

Brian Moses

Parent-Free Zone

Parents please note that from now on, our room is a 'Parent-Free Zone'.

There will be no spying under the pretence of tidying up.

There will be no banning of television programmes because our room is a tip.

No complaints about noise, or remarks about the ceiling caving in.

No disturbing the dirty clothes that have festered in piles for weeks.

MUM – WHY HAVEN'T YOU MADE OUR BEDS?

Brian Moses

A Hot Time In The Supermarket

When my mum gave my dad
The juiciest, most romantic kiss
Right there in the supermarket

And worse
Began to quickstep him down the aisle
To their favourite tune.

I couldn't believe it.
Everybody stared.
My cheeks began to burn.

In our basket
The hot chilli sauce sweated
Ice cream melted
Ten frozen fish fingers defrosted
The fizzy wine popped its cork
The tomato sauce went redder
The tinned salmon pinker
The cream of mushroom soup
Boiled over
And the chicken drumsticks
Beat out a tango.

I had to have
Three tins of pop from the cold shelf
Two ice lollies
And a big swig of natural spring water
Just to get over it.

David Harmer

Not The Dreaded Photo Album!

Parents! Huh!
Don't you just hate them?

You can guarantee that whenever we have visitors:
Uncle Fred, Auntie Ivy, Grandma Madge and Grandad Bill,
long lost Auntie Alice, or cousin Sidney twice removed
Mum and Dad will always, and I mean ALWAYS
get out the dreaded photo albums
and we have to sit through two and a half hours of
embarrassing snapshots of me . . .

stark naked in the bath with bubbles in my ears

cuddling a four foot pink fluffy teddy bear

sitting on my potty with my finger up my nose
and my nappy on my head

wearing chocolate cake like a balaclava,
cherries all over my face like extra alien eyes

the first time I tried to dress myself
with my shorts over my eyes and socks on my hands

dressed as a page boy at my Auntie's wedding
in a blue and white sailor suit and silly hat with ribbons

holding hands and kissing my posh cousin Tabatha
who has pink ribbons and flowery dresses
but never wipes her nose

blinking on every school photograph where it looks like
Mum cut my fringe with the crimping scissors

in the clothes that Mum and Dad bought me
thinking they were really trendy but were two years behind
and cheap off the market so it was okay

wearing that lovely woolly jumper that Nanna knitted
as a Christmas present using leftover wool
so that it had twenty-seven shades of green and brown
with a Thomas the Tank Engine motif
and the left arm was longer than the right.
It itched like crazy.

Everyone has a really good laugh
and I have to sit through it all tight lipped and red faced.
When I suggest that we look at last year's holiday snaps
where Mum won the knobbly knees contest
and Dad dressed up as an oven-ready turkey for the fancy dress
they tell me it's time I went to bed
and that our visitors wouldn't be interested anyway.

Parents! Huh!
Don't you just hate them?

Paul Cookson

HOW EMBARRASSING

14

Here Comes Another One of Dad's Famous Last Warnings

'I'm not going
to tell you
again,'

says Dad.
(Just before
he tells me
again.)

Bernard Young

Victoria's Poem

Send me upstairs without any tea,
refuse me a plaster to stick on my knee.

Make me kiss Grandpa who smells of his pipe,
make me eat beetroot, make me eat tripe.

Throw all my best dolls into the river.
Make me eat bacon and onions – with liver.

Tell Mr Allan I've been a bad girl,
rename me Nellie, rename me Pearl.

But don't, even if
the world suddenly ends
            ever again,
                Mother,
wipe my face with a tissue
in front of my friends.

Fred Sedgwick

Nag Nag Nag

Music – turn down
Socks – pick up
Room – tidy
Sister – play with
Answer back – don't even think about it
Consideration – have some
Know better – you should
Speak – when you're spoken to
Mouth full – don't talk with
Chores – first, play later
Piano – who wanted those lessons?
Muddy boots – not in here you don't
Feet – wipe
Friends – no homes to go to?
Computer games – you'll ruin your eyes

MUMBF!

Biscuits – none left
Hotel – you treat this house like a
Hamster – feed
Homework – now
Nose – wipe
Bath – please take one
Ears – wash behind
Teeth – clean
Lights – out
Sleep – tight.

Mum? Yes?
Rest – give it a.

Jane Wright

Smacking

Why do mums and dads
      SMACK?

Surely when they were young
their mums and dads
smacked them.
They must know how
it sends the heart
scurrying for cover,
how it stings
and flings the mind
into fear and flight.

So, why do mums and dads
      SMACK?

Try as I might
I cannot understand it.
One minute they say they love us.
It's all –
'Who's a booful boy then?'
but when things don't suit them
it's –
'If you don't watch out
I'll give you a clout.'

I reckon when I'm a dad
I'll be glad
to say –
'Here son, have £5 –
go get us an ice cream
and treat yourself
to something else –
and don't worry about your room
I'll run a hoover over it
while you're out
at the cinema.'

Yes, when I'm a dad
I'll never cuff or clout,
rant or rave,
scream and shout.

I'll build towers of Lego,
have forgiveness tattooed
on my tongue.

Pie Corbett

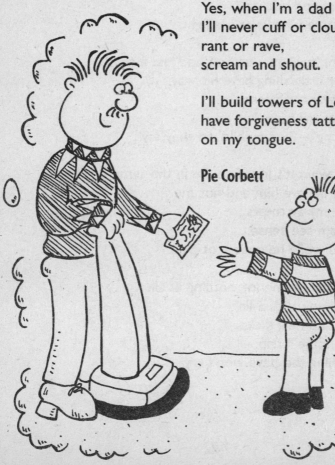

Always in the Wrong

I've got a problem that won't go away,
A problem I can't seem to solve.
I'm thirteen years old,
'Still a child' so I'm told —
Except when our John is involved.

At nine and a half he's younger by far,
But he's tall, and he's really quite bright.
And my parents can't see
That's it's him and not me
Who's to blame whenever we fight.

They say, 'You're grown up and he's just a child,
Let the poor little thing have his way.'
But when I want to spend
A few days at my friend's
I'm 'too young' — 'just a child' so they say.

You'll know what it's like if you're in the same boat,
They always believe him and not me.
And despite my attempts
To make them see sense,
I'm punished while he goes scot-free.

He'll say, 'Philip hit me for nothing at all.'
And yet he knows it's a lie.
He'll punch and he'll kick,
He'll push and he'll trip —
There's nothing the devil won't try.

It would just serve him right, if out of the blue
A new bouncing babe came along,
And then maybe he'll
Understand how it feels
To be right – yet still in the wrong.

Clive Webster

Chill Out, Dad!

Chill out, Dad.
Chill out.
Why don't you
take it easy?
There's no need
to scream and shout.

Try to be reasonable
Try to understand
Why do you always feel the need
To be totally in command?

Chill out, Dad.
Chill out.
Be cool. Life's
For living.
That's the golden rule.

Relax, sit back.
Get into the groove.
Get real, Dad.
You've got nothing to prove.

Chill out, Dad.
Chill out and listen
From time to time.
If you listened more often
We'd get on really fine. .

Try not to be so serious
You've forgotten how to smile.
Lie back, close your eyes
Take it easy for a while –

And CHILL OUT, DAD
just chill on out,
learn to let go.

Try not to get too worried
I'll teach you all you need to
know!

Tony Langham

Chinese Water Torture

Chinese Water Torture
Drip Drip Drip.
Can I, can I, Mum
Go on the trip trip trip?

Oh can I Mum? Please let me. Go on Mum –
Mum . . . pretty please?
I'll even go down on my bended
Knees knees knees.

I'll try wheedling and fawning
From day's end to new day dawning
I'll work on her all morning.
While she's waking, stretching, yawning.
I will plead and I will beg
Like a cat twined round her leg
Miaowing and miaowing for a feed.

I'll grumble up to bed
My question nagging in her head
Until she sees how very much I NEED.

Oh come on, Mum, I promise
I'll never, never ask,
For a single other thing my whole life long.
But I've really got to do this.
You just don't understand.
To stop me doing this is cruel. It's wrong.
Everyone will be there.
I'll be the only one
The lonely one that's left behind at home.

Can I, can I, Mum,
Go on the trip trip trip?
Chinese Water Torture
Drip Drip Drip.

Jan Dean

When You're a Child

When you're a child
you've got to do
the things that grown-ups
say to you.

They might be right
(I'm sure they're wrong!)
but you are young
and they are strong.

'Don't do that.
Do this,' they say.
You sulk or cry
and then obey.

You love them and
you hate them too
for all the things
they do to you.

Charles Thomson

When You're Grown Up

When you're grown up
with children too
you can get mad
at things they do.

I'm sure you're right
(never unjust) –
you tell them off
because you must.

'Not that,' you say,
'Here's what to do',
the way your parents
did to you.

And just as you
now praise or blame,
your children too
will do the same.

Charles Thomson

Roundabout

arguing with your parents
is like being on a roundabout

not one of the razz and jazz fun of the fair sort
one of grey tarmac grim with grinding traffic
one you're going round and round
shut in the car
with the windows closed
going round and round
past all the exit roads
and no one can agree
which one to take

round and round
the map's no use
will you go to Give In or Get Your Own Way?
is there a decent road to Compromise?
some are clearly marked Dead End, others
may end in hopeless confusion or lead to endless detours
that will bring you back just where you started

going round and round
and no one really knows the way out
and the baby's been sick
and everyone's shouting
and the car's swerving this way and that
because everyone wants
to turn the wheel, press the accelerator,
stamp on the brakes
all at the same time
arms and legs and voices flailing wildly

round and round
with the rain battering down
till the family finally lurches off
down one road or another
with nobody sure
that you've gone the right way

Dave Calder

Tomb Tunes

Here lies the body
Of a poor, tired Dad,
Driven by his children
Crazy, mad.

Here lies the body
Of a worn-out Mum,
Moaned at, overworked,
Ignored, glum.

Here lies the body
Of an only child,
Peevish, selfish,
Reckless wild.

Here lies the body
Of a ten year-old;
Didn't do
As he was told.

Here lie the bodies
Of family folk,
Kind and loving –
Must be a joke!

John Kitching

All Right, Mum?

I do like your dress, Mum,
it's trendy, and it's cool,
but I'd wear jeans, if I were you,
to meet me from school.

Can you come in Dad's car?
It's not that yours is bad,
but the stickers in the windows
are a bit sad.

I love the way you've done your hair,
but I should wear a scarf.
No, I don't think it's funny
but my friends might laugh.

Your make-up rather suits you.
You know I'm really glad
my best friend told me yesterday
that I look like my dad.

Of course I'm really proud of you.
I'm not at all ashamed,
and if they ask 'Whose mother's that?'
I can't be blamed.

Celia Warren

Parents!

Parents!
They're so embarrassing.

When my dad sneezes,
He makes such a racket
It's as if a minor explosion
Has been detonated
Inside his nose.
Then he whips out
His handkerchief with a flourish
And trumpets loudly,
Shattering the silence
With his coughing, spluttering and wheezing.

As for my mum,
Her stomach gurgles and rumbles
Like a broken cistern
That never stops filling.
It saves the loudest churnings
For that moment's silence
In the middle of a concert
Or the most dramatic moment
At the climax of a play,
So people turn and frown
Or pretend not to notice,
Though they couldn't help but have heard.
And I go bright red,
Wishing the ground would open up
And swallow me,
Or that I was cool and confident enough
To look disdainful,
As if to say:
She's not my mum, you know,
Don't blame me!

Parents!
They're so embarrassing.

John Foster

Fair Play?

Don't swear!
said my father.
I don't want to hear it.
Where the hell do you get it from?
Just *where?*

Lipstick!
said my mother.
I don't want to see it.
And where's *my* orange lipstick gone?
Nightmare!

Smoking!
said my parents.
We don't want to smell it.
And don't you touch *our* fags again.
Don't dare!

Judith Nicholls

Please Don't Answer Me Back Dad

Please don't answer me back Dad,
I'm trying to keep my cool;
You shouldn't need telling twice Dad,
don't treat me like a fool.
    Time after time, day after day,
    I have to put up with this stuff;
    You'd better buck your ideas up Dad,
    I've just about had enough.

Please don't answer me back Dad,
I've told you the way it is;
And stop asking silly questions,
What is this, a flippin' quiz?
    Over and over, again and again,
    You're pushing me too far;
    Don't come the high and mighty with me,
    Who do you think you are?

Please don't answer me back Dad,
You're starting to make me cross;
You can slam the door and sulk all you like,
I couldn't give a toss.
    You've always got something to nag about,
    Then you fly into a rage;
    So there's just one thing I've got to say to you,
    It's about time you acted your age.

Mike Jubb

Wash Your Mouth Out

If I ever came home
and bad-mouthed Mum,
she'd say that she ought
to wash out my mouth
with soap and water.

I'd laugh and say
she never would,
couldn't catch hold
or keep me still
for long enough.

Till one day she caught me
unawares, I came downstairs
and turned to find
both Dad and Mum
with soap and a sponge.

Dad gripped my shoulder
till I yelled and then,
quick as lightning, Mum forced
the sponge into my mouth
and twisted it round.

I choked on carbolic
and heard Dad say, 'Let that
be a lesson, just don't bring home
all those nasty words
that you learn in the street

42

or you can expect the same
treatment again.'
And I lunged upstairs
to try to find some aniseed ball
or double strength mint,

something to mask the awful taste
that was worse than mustard,
or medicine, while I muttered
those words that I learnt in the street
over and over again.

Brian Moses

Purple Shoes

Mum and me had a row yesterday,
a big, exploding
howdareyouspeaktomelikethatI'mofftostayatGran's
kind of row.

It was about shoes.
I'd seen a pair of purple ones at Carter's,
heels not too high, soft suede, silver buckles;
'No' she said.
'Not suitable for school.
I can't afford to buy rubbish.'
That's when we had our row.

I went to bed longing for those shoes.
They made footsteps in my mind,
kicking up dance dust;
I wore them in my dreams across a shiny floor,
under flashing coloured lights.
It was ruining my life not to have them.

This morning they were mine.
Mum relented and gave me the money.
I walked out of the store wearing new purple shoes.
I kept seeing myself reflected in shop windows
with purple shoes on,
walking to the bus stop,
walking the whole length of our street
wearing purple shoes.

On Monday I shall go to school in purple shoes.
Mum will say no a thousand furious times
But I don't care.
I'm not going to give in.

Irene Rawnsley

Walking the Dog Seems Like Fun to Me

I said, The dog wants a walk.

Mum said to Dad, It's your turn.
Dad said, I always walk the dog.
Mum said, Well I walked her this morning.
Dad said, She's your dog.
I didn't want a dog in the first place.

Mum said, It's your turn.

Dad stood up and threw the remote control
at the pot plant.
Dad said, I'm going down the pub.
Mum said, Take the dog.

Dad shouted, No way!
Mum shouted, You're going nowhere!

I grabbed Judy's lead
and we both bolted out the back door.

The stars were shining like diamonds.
Judy sniffed at a hedgehog, rolled up in a ball.
She ate a discarded kebab on the pavement.
She tried to chase a cat that ran up a tree.

Walking the dog
seems like fun to me.

Roger Stevens

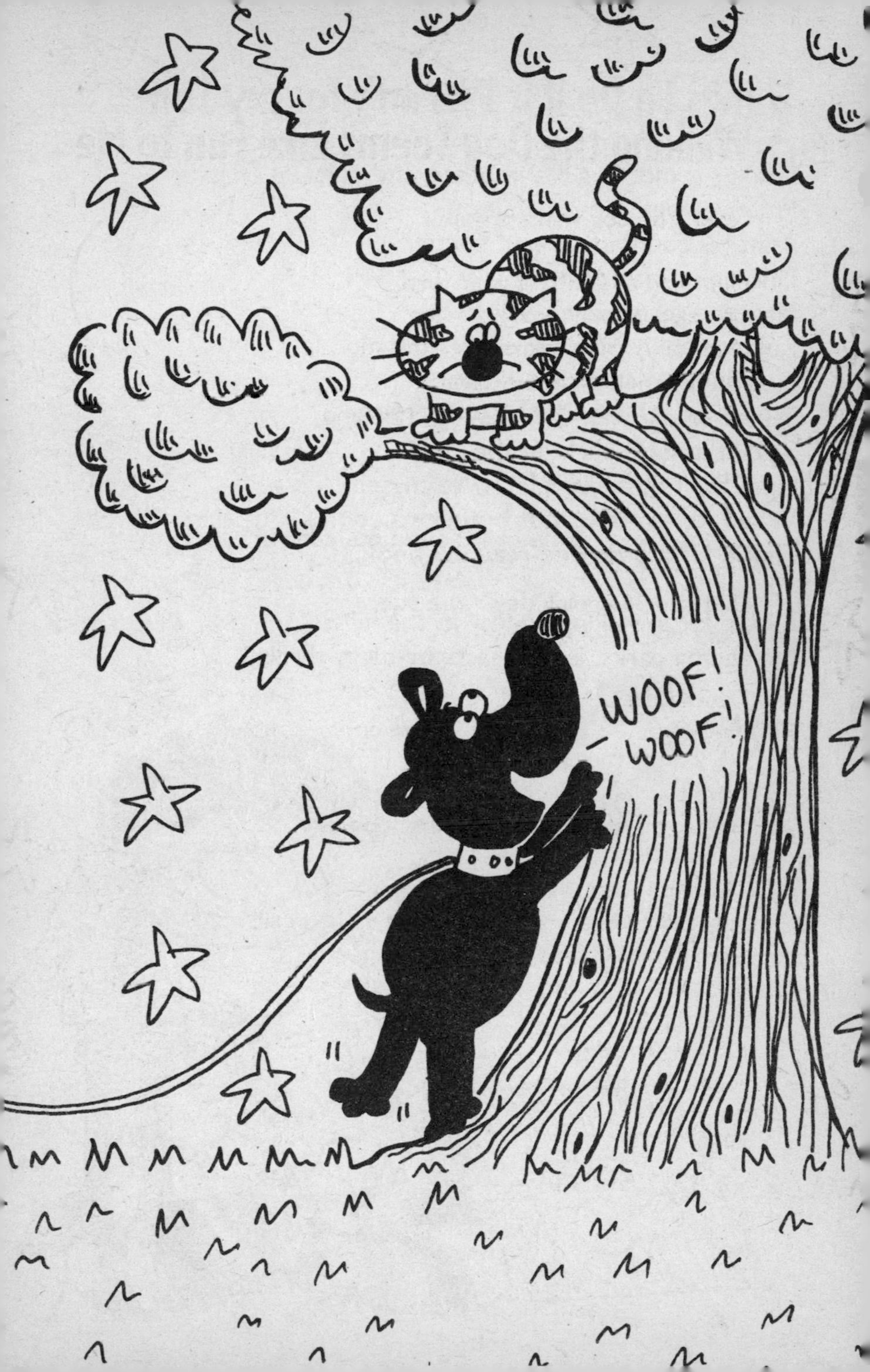
WOOF!
WOOF!

Things I'd Do if it Weren't for my Son

Drink my morning tea in peace and quiet.
Practice yoga. Go on a diet.
Paint his room in almond white.
Dismantle the strobe light.
Give the gerbil cage away.
Keep the telly off all day.
Get the kitchen nice and clean.
Take a break from the washing machine.
Stack the CDs back on the shelf.
Have the house completely to myself.
When it's tea-time, not bother to cook.
Phone for a pizza and read my book.

PS Go for a walking holiday in the hills.
No theme parks, laser quests or mega thrills.

Tony Mitton

Things I'd Do if it Weren't for Mum

Live on cola, crisps and cake.
Trade the gerbil for a snake.
Fall asleep in front of the telly.
Only wash when I'm really smelly.
Leave my clothes all scattered about.
Play loud music, scream and shout.
Do what I feel like with my hair.
Throw tantrums. Belch loud. Swear.
Paint my bedroom red and black.
Leave the dishes in a stack.
Find out what it's like to be me.
Let this list grow long . . . Get free!

PS Take my savings in my hand.
Buy a ticket to Laserland.

Tony Mitton

BOOM!
BANG!

Divorce

I did not promise
to stay with you till death us do part, or
anything like that,
so part I must, and quickly. There are things
I cannot suffer
any longer: Mother, you have never, ever, said
a kind word
or a thank you for all the tedious chores I have done;
Father, your breath
smells like a camel's and gives me the hump;
all you ever say is:
'Are you off in the cream puff, Lady Muck?'
In this day and age?
I would be better off in an orphanage.

HOW CAN THEY BE RELATED TO ME?

I want a divorce.
There are parents in the world whose faces turn
up to the light
who speak in the soft murmur of rivers
and never shout.
There are parents who stroke their children's cheeks
in the dead night
and sing in the colourful voices of rainbows,
red to blue.
These parents are not you. I never chose you.
You are rough and wild,
I don't want to be your child. All you do is shout
and that's not right.
I will file for divorce in the morning at first light.

Jackie Kay

Daft Questions Deserve Daft Answers

Matt Simpson

EVER AFTER